The

Awesome Life

Series

Your Awesome Life!

90 Ways To Add MORE
Awesome Every Day

Volume 1, Edition 1

Jen Appreneur and Trish Rock

The "Awesome Life" Series presented by Awesome Publications.com

The purpose of this book is to entertain and educate by considering the experiences of others. You should always rely on your own independent professional advice before undertaking any new venture. No warranties or assurances, guarantees or representations about the accuracy, reliability or timelines or otherwise of the information contained in the book can be given. To the fullest extent permitted by law, Awesome Publications (including the authors and editors) shall not be liable (including liability for negligence) for any loss or damage arising out of your use of this book. You should always consider the appropriateness of the information in this book having regard to your relevant personal circumstances.

All events and scenarios in this book are based upon the author's and/or contributor's experience and are true and correct at the time of writing. Some contributions have been sourced openly from public information sites on the internet. No claims or warranties or ownerships or royalties are or shall be paid.

Published and Distributed by Awesome Publications, www.AwesomePublications.com

PO Box 544 Williamstown Victoria 3016 (Melbourne) Australia

Phone: +61 3 9397 3975
Facsimile: +613 9397 3394
Email: info@awesomepublications.com
Website: www.AwesomePublications.com

ISBN: 978-0-646-92111-2 (paperback)

ISBN: 978-0-646-92098-6 (ePub)

loans that change lives

In an effort to support self-sustainability, innovation and entrepreneurial creativity, we fund Kiva loans. Join our team and help change lives, for as little as a $25 loan. More info at: www.kiva.org/team/AwesomeEntrepreneurs.

DEDICATION

To Inspired Entrepreneurs and Authors all over the world who have awesome messages that improve peoples' lives.

May you live <u>your</u> most awesome life and remember to celebrate everything.

TABLE OF CONTENTS

Join our
"Awesome Source"

INSPIRED NEWS

Mail list

**90 Days <u>FREE</u> Membership
SPECIAL OFFER for you!**

FOREWORD

How Two *'Clazy-Ladies'* Made <u>AWESOME</u> The New Sexy

On a train ride to a Life and Business Seminar in Melbourne, Australia, March 2014, two business colleagues and girlfriends Trish and Jen, were discussing how their (your) perspective ON life affects your experiences IN life. And that in full awareness, even the bad things that happen, if turned in to learning, possess positivity and even blessings for better-ness rather than bitterness and therefore a more vibrant and joyful life.

The idea of living from a position of positivity, knowing there's always something good that can come out of any situation was what they were really saying. They discussed the idea of *"What if we looked at everything happening in our lives as being awesome ... eventually?"* That would mean there was always reason to celebrate and always opportunities to be grateful. It's all actually just a matter of conscious choice to create an inner energy or sense of awesomeness.

In their inspired (and excited) state, they had a joint epiphany to share with the world - that anyone can create an awesome life simply by creating awesome energy within yourself first, which in turn improves every situation and circumstance in your outer life.

They knew they had lots of friends on social media that have lots of awesome thoughts and ideas too. So, by using online crowd-sourcing facilities, they invited everyone they knew to contribute an awesome thought to a compilation book.

The book is designed for you to use on a daily basis - to easily invoke and activate the energy of awesomeness in to your life every day. This increase in your energy will in turn, bring greater happiness (and awesomeness) to other people around you too.

The true power of activating the energy in the thoughts shared in this book is alike to a 'wave of awesomeness' sweeping across the world.

The response to this idea was overwhelming and before they knew it, the book had grown twice as big as they had originally planned so once again, they got together for a 'ride', this time over Skype and brainstormed out how to make it work now that the inclusion of other people made the power bigger than first thought.

What came out of that second meeting was what you see now, a 90 day plan to integrate and activate awesomeness in to your life.

And, as both Trish and Jen are mobile app designers, they added in an app of awesomeness (why not!) so that every day you can receive awesome thoughts right there on your mobile device. The app also includes meditations and focus visuals to help embody the thoughts of awesomeness in to your being and life.

There will be 4 Volumes produced, each being 90 ways of awesome thoughts to activate awesomeness over a full year in your life. Once you're fully activated, life will never be the same.

Well, this story and the vision do not end there. The 4 book Volumes and the mobile app form part of a much bigger plan – to help people create your *"Year of Living Awesomely"*. You can find out more about that on their website www.AwesomeSourceNews.com.

You can also find out more about their public talks and workshops and "The Year of Living Awesomely, Bus of Love Tour" on the website along with links for the mobile app, merchandise and more opportunities for you to be involved in more ways too.

For now, read the Introduction and get started on Day 1 of Your MORE Awesome Life!

PS: You may wonder about "Clazy-Ladies" in the headline – it's a term they phrased during a business trip to Thailand that they took. They will tell you it's an abbreviation for "Classy, Crazy Ladies" and every time they hear it, you'll hear a little giggle from them. And if you add AWESOME to the front of it, you'll definitely get their attention.

ABOUT THE AUTHORS / CO-CREATORS

Meet Jen Appreneur

Jen is a digital age entrepreneur and businesswoman – publishing, books, audios, videos, webinars and software on today's leading digital mediums.

These include mobile apps, social media, blogging/internet & electronic magazines.

In addition, she offers online training courses and runs regular live training events in Australia, the USA and UK too occasionally.

A successful web entrepreneur since 1996, she has owned over 150 different web businesses, selling both instant download digital products and 'on-consignment' physical products - generating millions of dollars of sales for more than a decade - a formidable record by comparison to many others offering education, tools and systems for marketing success.

Current business ventures include:

- The "Queendom of Wealth™" – A High-end Mentoring Program, Mobile App, Digital Magazine, Board game, Range of Merchandise and live networking events to teach women fast and fun ways to build financial independence and to create professional fulfillment.

- "Mobile App System™" – An app design company that ensures apps for business include and are integrated in to cash-flow systems. The business is now licensed and assists service providers to expand in to the app development industry, use an easy-to-do app-building platform.

She's also a multiple-time, international best-selling Author, a sought-after public speaker around the world and media presenter.

She says, *"A little-known secret to AWESOME business success is collaboration. An idea known by many but used effectively by only a few. This book shows you how you can do it effectively too."*

You can find out more about Jen at: www.QueendomOfWealth.com

Meet Trish Rock

Trish is an entrepreneur and a modern day businesswoman who has embraced the digital age of communication and relationship building.

In retail business since 1989, and now working online, Trish believes the key to success is the experience you can give to your customers.

She has written 2 books that teach this business philosophy as well as a home study course, audio products and a webinar series. She has also contributed to 6 books on business, social media and mindset and writes a regular column on business, marketing and mobile app technology for a global magazine and a national magazine.

Trish has won awards for design excellence as well as outstanding business achievement and growth. She is a sought after app designer and developer as well as a speaker and media presenter with a following in social media and blogging.

She says *"I believe everyone can have an AWESOME business and life if they can first believe it to be true of themselves."*

You can find out more about Trish at:
www.StrategicBusinessApps.com

INTRODUCTION

"Once upon a time I tried to be Perfect, then I realized that being Awesome was so much more fun!"

It's true! We all strive towards a version of 'perfect' in our life.

Whether it's a version of perfect we've created in our own mind, or a version imposed on you by other people in your life and/or probably a combination of both, there's a vision or idea of what you are working towards.

And sometimes, the pressure we put on ourselves in striving to achieve our idea of a perfect life is unnecessary and in fact it can actually deplete our energy or life force.

When you ponder that, it's kind of ironic isn't it – that we strive towards a vision of some ideal or perfect result in our life, yet the very process to achieve that can leave us far from fulfilled and actually, even feeling exhausted and incomplete. It's a long way from feeling awesome every day that's for sure!

When asked *"What thing about humanity surprises you the most?"* the XIV Dalai Lama answered:

"Man.... Because he sacrifices his health in order to make money. Then he sacrifices money to recuperate his health. And then he is so anxious about the future that he does not enjoy the present; the result being that he does not live in the present

or the future; he lives as if he is never going to die, and then dies having never really lived."

It's a powerful statement and a truth for many in today's fast-paced life.

And we agree with The Dalai Lama – and we thought his quote was awesome enough to be in this book!

Your life, no matter how imperfect it may seem to you is already awesome, whether you fully realize it yourself yet or not. There's so much to celebrate, including even the little things that often go un-noticed in day-to-day life.

And no matter how awesome your life may feel right now, let's say it was measured on an awesomeness scale of 1-10, this quirky little book of inspired quotes is going to help you to consciously connect with more awesomeness in more ways, each day for the next 90 days.

Over the next 90 days, we will guide through a series of inspired thoughts – ideas if you like, in the form of short quotes that have been written and submitted by awesome entrepreneurs from around the world who want to help you to increase your sense of awesomeness in each aspect, every day, of your life.

To build a greater awareness and consciousness of awesomeness, the short quotes have been organized in to Chapters in this book. Each of the seven Chapters represents a different aspect of life energy and experience and you will be invited to read one quote each day (starting with the first quote in the first Chapter) and ponder its relevance in your awesome life, as your life exists right now.

By finding the connection (the awareness), you'll raise your consciousness of celebrating that awesomeness and subsequently, allow an expansion in your conscious thoughts for more awesomeness in each of the seven life aspects or realms.

It will be like a stimulating and energizing workout for your mind that will permeate and integrate in to your heart consciousness and flow through and activate in to each and every cell of your entire body.

By working through the 90 Days with us, you will become more and more of a human embodiment of awesomeness. That's pretty exciting really and that is the very experience we have had in raising our awareness and aligning our consciousness with the life force or energy and experience of awesomeness.

The more aligned we become, through recognition of where we are at presently, the more awesomeness has opened up to us. It's quite remarkable AND a lot of fun really.

As well as having more fun, integrating celebration in to our daily life, whether it's expressed inwardly, outwardly or both, makes the idea of celebrating everything feel and become so much more natural. And it may even become obvious to you just how much the idea of celebrating everything has been missing in your life until now.

Once you connect to the energy of 'Your Awesome Life' force, you feel so much more powerful, and you will gain a greater sense of possibility of how much more powerful you become.

These short quotes are supported by meditations and inspiration instructions in our mobile app. We encourage you to download it and use the book and the app together, to get the absolute most out of it. (More info on the accompanying mobile app is on our Other Resources page at the back of this book).

We hope you love all of what we have created for you so much that you'll continue on after these first 90 days and join us on the "Year of Living Awesomely" Project too. (More info on our Facebook Group that you are now invited to join is on our Other Resources page at the back of this book).

As mentioned above, this book contains inspired and very awesome quotes from entrepreneurs all around the globe. They have contributed their best or most favorite quotes to this book to help expand your thoughts and increase your awesomeness energy and life force.

Feel free to reach out to any or all of them, either through our Facebook community or individually. We have provided their name and a link to their website below their contribution as well as in the Bibliography.

It's time now to get started with Chapter 1 and Quote 1 to energize your current awesome thought patterns, stimulate new awesome thought patterns and release old un-awesome thought patterns to raise your awareness and align your conscious thoughts with more awesomeness.

By following the instructions below, the process will help you become a greater embodiment of awesomeness –which in turn will draw more awesomeness in to your physical life and create more awesomeness in the world.

Adding more awesomeness to yourself and to all around you is a pretty cool way to live and plenty of reasons to celebrate life!

Oh one last thing, to follow us online and connect to our work at any time, these are our two most favorite social media hash-tags:
- #awesomelife
- #celebrateeverything.

How to use this book for maximum awesomeness

There are a number of ways you can use this book, not just how we suggest. Our guideline for how to use it is based on a process to a powerful outcome.

Our process is designed to help you evolve your sense of awesomeness in your life, as it is right now through this process:

THE
'YOUR AWESOME LIFE™'
ACTIVATION SYSTEM

Raise Awareness --->> Align Consciousness --->> Activate Embodiment

At the start of the day:
Open the book to the page you are currently at (use a sticky note or digital bookmark so you can easily find the next one each day).

Step 1 – Raise Awareness

- Read the quote silently to yourself at normal pace.
- Pause for 5-10 seconds and take a deep breath or two at this time
- Read the quote silently to yourself again, this time at half normal pace.

As you read it at half-pace, take notice of each word by looking at it more intentionally but still read it in a manner that allows the words to flow in to each other and form a continuing sentence or paragraph.

Do not read a word, then pause, read a word, then pause too slowly otherwise you will lose the rhythm and overall meaning. Just slow it down from your normal reading pace. If you have not read at half normal pace before, you may find this a little unusual but you will soon get the hang of it.

You can practice pace by becoming conscious of your 'normal' reading pace, your 'fast' reading pace and your 'slow' reading pace.

We often read slower to children – this is the pace you want to achieve, as if you were reading it to children. Repeat this as many times as you feel you want to or need to so that it feels like it's at a pace that's comfortable for you.

Step 2 – Align Consciousness

- Take a slow, deep breath in, hold it momentarily and then exhale at the same slower pace.
- Read the quote out loud to yourself at slow pace.
- Repeat this 2-3 times, or more if you want to. Take a slow, deep breath in and before you read it out each time.

Step 3 – Activate Embodiment

- Take out your "Your Awesome Life™" journal (or a notebook or use the notepad in the app) and write out or type the quote yourself.
- Ask yourself this question "How does this quote relate or reflect in my current life?"
- Below the quote, list at least 3 ways this quote relates or reflects in your life right now. List the ways as they spring in to your mind.

You do not need to organize your thoughts, just write them down. There are no right or wrong answers, just what comes to mind. By writing or typing them out, you create a record to refer back to later and also to build on as more ideas come to you later – and they will, later on the day of the quote and maybe at a future random time as well.

It's pretty awesome how our mind and body work together to create ideas that flow. In some cases, you may, initially, struggle to make the connection of a quote to your current life, especially if it's about something that does not appear to be in your life right now.

For example, you may not be a parent but there's a quote about parenting. This is where you expand your thinking of the definition of parenting. Parenting may mean Leadership to you – so you can think about the quote in the format of guiding yourself (self governance or parenting) or guiding/leading a business or a community (group governance). It is this expansive thinking that will help you make the connections and create the embodiment of the awesome energy of each quote.

- Now list at least 3 new ways you can introduce the idea of the quote (the awesome energy of it) in to your life.
- Read either to yourself silently or out loud, the 3 new ways as a sentence or paragraph, starting with *"Today I introduce 3 new ways of awesomeness. They are ……………"* (Read them in the order you have written or typed them out).

You can revisit and repeat these processes for each quote as many times on the day as you want to and of course add to them at any time over the next 90 days. You can also work on more than one quote on any one day, especially if you feel inspired or are seeking new inspiration. Just make sure you complete the process for one quote through the 3 steps before starting on the second, third and beyond.

If you have any questions or comments and especially if you have some AWESOMENESS to share with us by completing the process, please visit us at our Facebook Group. Details are in the Other Resources section at the back of this book.

Finally, if there's one message we hope to impress and leave you with, it's this:

"Life gets awesome when you make up your mind to perceive it as being awesome. Celebrate everything!"

Jen and Trish

Join our
"Awesome Source"
INSPIRED NEWS
Mail list

90 Days <u>FREE</u> Membership
SPECIAL OFFER for you!

Go to

www.AwesomeSourceNews.com

Right Now

CHAPTER 1

Awesome BEING

DEFINITION:

BEING is physical presence.

Establishing security and stability while building the foundations in business and life.

These quotes will give you an awareness and consciousness about the importance of taking grounded action to manifest material abundance, in a more awesome way.

THE
'YOUR AWESOME LIFE™'
ACTIVATION SYSTEM

Refer to the Introduction for full details.

Step 1 – Raise Your Awareness

Step 2 – Align Your Consciousness

Step 3 – Activate Your Embodiment.

First, have a definite, clear practical ideal, a goal, an objective. Second, have the necessary means to achieve your ends, wisdom, money, materials and methods. Third, adjust all your means to that end.

- Aristotle

THIS AWESOME QUOTE FROM:

Aristotle

www.en.wikipedia.org/wiki/Aristotle

66

Some people say the glass is half full, while others say it is half empty.

I say...just show me the tap!

99

- Sam Usher

THIS AWESOME QUOTE FROM:

Sam Usher
Adventure Philosopher
www.AdventurePhilosopher.com

> **"**
>
> *Falling down is a part of life.*
> *Getting back up is living.*
>
> **"**
>
> - Georgina Helliwell

THIS AWESOME QUOTE FROM:

Georgina Helliwell

www.facebook.com/AnimalAlchemy

> 66
>
> *Speed is useful only if you are running in the right direction.*
>
> 99
>
> - Joel Barker

THIS AWESOME QUOTE FROM:

Joel Barker

www.JoelBarker.com

> ❝
>
> *Do you cut and paste your past or create a new life today?*
>
> ❞
>
> - Jutta Klipsch

THIS AWESOME QUOTE FROM:

Jutta Klipsch

JuttaKlipsch@gmail.com

66

Definitiveness of purpose is the starting point of all achievement.

- W. Clement Stone

THIS AWESOME QUOTE FROM:

W. Clement Stone

www.en.wikipedia.org/wiki/W._Clement_Stone

66

When sleeping women wake, mountains move!

99

- Chinese Proverb

THIS AWESOME QUOTE FROM:

Heather Passant
Love, Courage and Relationship Coach
www.LifeHarmony.com.au

> 66
>
> *You have a choice in the way you view potential or lack of opportunity in the day ahead. No matter what happened, you can either be an optimist or a pessimist.*
>
> 99
>
> - Tracie O'Keefe

THIS AWESOME QUOTE FROM:

Tracie O'Keefe

www.InspirationForSurviveandProsper.com/book

> **"**
>
> *When everything seems to be going against you, remember that the airplane takes off against the wind, not with it.*
>
> **"**
>
> - Henry Ford

THIS AWESOME QUOTE FROM:

Henry Ford

www.en.wikipedia.org/wiki/Henry_ford

> **66**
>
> *There is no scarcity of opportunity to make a living at what you love, there's only scarcity of resolve to make it happen.*
>
> **99**
>
> - Wayne Dyer

THIS AWESOME QUOTE FROM:

Leisa Hunter Smith

www.LeisaSmith.com

> **"**
>
> *Connect to the Mother Earth daily. Being grounded enables better decisions in business and life for a more prosperous outcome.*
>
> **"**
>
> - Trish Rock

THIS AWESOME QUOTE FROM:

Trish Rock

www.AwesomePublications.com

> *Start where you are. Use what you have. Do what you can.*
>
> - Arthur Ashe

THIS AWESOME QUOTE FROM:

Arthur Ashe

www.en.wikipedia.org/wiki/Arthur_ashe

There are risks and costs to a program of action, but they are far less than the long-range risks and costs of comfortable inaction.

- John F Kennedy

THIS AWESOME QUOTE FROM:

Lorraine Enright

www.CertitudeLifeCoaching.com.au

CHAPTER 2

Awesome FEELING

DEFINITION:

FEELING is creative connection and relationships.

These quotes will give you an awareness and consciousness about the importance of self worth, inspired creativity and making decisions while taking action from an empowered emotional position, for more awesome relationships.

THE
'YOUR AWESOME LIFE™'
ACTIVATION SYSTEM

Refer to the Introduction for full details.

Step 1 – Raise Your Awareness

Step 2 – Align Your Consciousness

Step 3 – Activate Your Embodiment.

> *Confidence is arriving at self awareness and self acceptance.*
>
> *It's not something that you do, it's who you are.*
>
> - Anfernee Chansamooth

THIS AWESOME QUOTE FROM:

Anfernee Chansmooth

www.Confidentpreneur.com

> **"**
>
> *Life wasn't meant to be easy. It was meant to be full of challenges and adventure to ensure you reach your full potential.*
>
> *Embrace your awesomeness.*
>
> **"**
>
> - Kathie Holmes

THIS AWESOME QUOTE FROM:

Kathie Holmes

www.CreativeAbilityNetwork.com

> "There is nothing more beautiful than a warrior woman standing in her power, courage, and confidence. From this place of strength, she is capable of loving the world in a way that transforms pain into promise...and hell into heaven."
>
> - Debbie Ford

THIS AWESOME QUOTE FROM:

Heather Passant
Love, Courage & Relationship Coach
www.LifeHarmony.com.au

> **"**
>
> *Just as a tide ebbs and flows, change and challenges come and go.*
>
> **"**
>
> - Allan 'Big Al' Connolly

THIS AWESOME QUOTE FROM:

Allan Connolly

www.BigAlConnolly.info

> *Life is a game, play full out and make it awesome!*
>
> - An Coppens

THIS AWESOME QUOTE FROM:

An Coppens

www.GamificationNation.com

> **"**
>
> *If you are not willing to risk the unusual, you will have to settle for the ordinary.*
>
> **"**
>
> - Jim Rohn

THIS AWESOME QUOTE FROM:

Maree Crosbie

www.MareeCrosbie.com

"

Nurturing my skills and talents makes me an even more awesome mum than I already am.

"

- Emma Perrow

THIS AWESOME QUOTE FROM:

Emma Perrow

www.SimpleFitness.com.au

> ❝
>
> *I want to be ME.*
>
> *Not the ME you think I should be. Not the ME my husband thinks I should be. Not the ME my children think I should be.*
>
> *I just want to be the ME I think I should be.*
>
> ❞
>
> - Cheryl Pollock

THIS AWESOME QUOTE FROM:

Cheryl Pollock

www.LiveLaughLoveCoaching.com.au

> "
>
> *You can't get swept off your feet if you are sitting down!*
>
> *Stand up and be noticed!*
>
> "
>
> - Claire Camden-Burch

THIS AWESOME QUOTE FROM:

Claire Camden-Burch

www.facebook.com/AlignmentAffirmations

> 66
>
> *...In our darkest moments, if we allow our creative selves expression, we can often touch something far greater than ourselves and begin to let the light in. Everyone is an artist. Creativity is your birthright and gives voice to your soul.*
>
> 99
>
> - Trypheyna McShane

THIS AWESOME QUOTE FROM:

Trypheyna McShane

www.IntimacyOfDeathAndDying.com

"

Out there in some garage is an entrepreneur who's forging a bullet you're your company's name on it.

"

- Gary Hamel

THIS AWESOME QUOTE FROM:

Gary Hamel

www.GaryHamel.com

"

I give myself permission to be happy now. I give myself permission to receive now. I give myself permission to be abundant now. I give myself permission to receive love now. I open my arms and allow myself permission to receive.

"

- Melissa Gibbons

THIS AWESOME QUOTE FROM:

Melissa Gibbons

www.AngelicEarth.com.au

> *Release the toxic stew of judgments, opinions and shadow beliefs, embracing NEW POSSIBILITIES wrapped up with gifts of wisdom and self worth.*
>
> - Heather Passant

THIS AWESOME QUOTE FROM:

Heather Passant
Love, Courage and Relationship Coach
www.LifeHarmony.com.au

CHAPTER 3

Awesome WILLPOWER

DEFINITION:

WILLPOWER is energy, YOUR powerful and positive energy.

These quotes will give you an awareness and consciousness about the importance of personal power and the will to keep moving forward in an empowered and effective way so as to enjoy more innate happiness in an awesome personal identity.

**THE
'YOUR AWESOME LIFE™'
ACTIVATION SYSTEM**

Refer to the Introduction for full details.

Step 1 – Raise Your Awareness

Step 2 – Align Your Consciousness

Step 3 – Activate Your Embodiment.

The world is a stimulus for inspiration ... reach out and then, go within.

- Chris Georgopoulos

THIS AWESOME QUOTE FROM:

Chris Georgopoulos

www.DiscoverYourInnerGem.com

> *Excuses keep your focus and energy in the past!*
>
> - Heather Passant

THIS AWESOME QUOTE FROM:

Heather Passant
Love, Courage and Relationship Coach
www.LifeHarmony.com.au

66

Being present is a present.

99

- Roula

THIS AWESOME QUOTE FROM:

Roula

www.PicsByRoula.com

> *I'm smarter today than I was yesterday, because I learned something new and I gave myself permission to grow.*
>
> - Heather James

THIS AWESOME QUOTE FROM:

Heather James, Inspiring Mums®
"Where Mums Smile & Shine®"
www.InspiringMums.com.au

"

Life's journey is not to arrive at the grave safely in a well preserved body, but rather to skid in sideways, totally worn out, shouting "Holy Shit ……. What an awesome ride!

"

- Author Unknown

THIS AWESOME QUOTE FROM:

Donna Mahoney

www.Innatepd.com

"

The only obstacle between you and your dream…is YOU.

"

- Ana Hall

THIS AWESOME QUOTE FROM:

Ana Hall

http://Anahall.Wordpress.com

> *No one has the right to tell you what you can or cannot do in your own life. No one has the right to tell you what is possible for you to achieve in your own life. No one has the right to stop you from achieving your dreams and goals. The only person stopping you is YOU.*
>
> - Nicole Torrens

THIS AWESOME QUOTE FROM:

Nicole Torrens

www.NicoleTorrens.com

> *I like who I AM.*
> *I like who I am BEING.*
> *I like who I have BECOME.*
>
> - Trish Rock

THIS AWESOME QUOTE FROM:

Trish Rock

www.AwesomePublications.com

"

*A product is a mere object.
A brand however has
personality. It is the
emotions you evoke, the
thoughts, the feelings and
the expectations created.
Protect it, love and nurture
it at all costs.*

"

- Melissa Robson

THIS AWESOME QUOTE FROM:

Melissa Robson

www.DivineCreative.com.au

My attitude will change yours! ®

- Heather James

THIS AWESOME QUOTE FROM:

Heather James, Inspiring Mums®
"Where Mums Smile & Shine®"
www.InspiringMums.com.au

> *Your most important legacy is your kids.*
>
> *Be a role model so your kids can pass on their experience and create generational change by raising loving, well-rounded kids*

\- John Edwards

THIS AWESOME QUOTE FROM:

John Edwards

www.ParentConsciously.com

> **"**
>
> *You can lead a horse to water. All you can do when you get it there is drown it. For the behavior you want from others can only be modeled by you. So while loving encouragement will bring its own rewards, forcing another will only succeed in killing the horse.*
>
> **"**
>
> - Phoebe Dangerfield

THIS AWESOME QUOTE FROM:

Phoebe Dangerfield

www.MindBizNiz.com.au

66

If you do what you have always done, you'll get what you've always gotten.

99

- Tony Robbins

THIS AWESOME QUOTE FROM:

Tony Robbins

www.TonyRobbins.com

> **"**
>
> *Today and onwards, I stand proud, for the bridges I've climbed, for the battles I've won, and for the examples I've set, but most importantly, for the person I have become.*
>
> *I like who I am now, finally, at peace with me.*
>
> **"**
>
> - Heather James

THIS AWESOME QUOTE FROM:

Heather James
"Where Mums Smile & Shine®"
www.InspiringMums.com.au

Download the

"Your Awesome Life!"

Mobile App

For 'on the go'
inspiration as well as:

Meditations to
'Activate Your Awesomeness' whenever
needed.

Available now at
iTunes, Google Play and Amazon app
stores

CHAPTER 4

Awesome LOVE

DEFINITION:

LOVE is understanding, trust and openness towards life, yourself and others.

These quotes will give you an awareness and consciousness about the importance of the power of trust in your heart as well as forgiveness and compassion in everyday living, to enjoy a more awesome loving and balanced life.

THE
'YOUR AWESOME LIFE™'
ACTIVATION SYSTEM

Refer to the Introduction for full details.

Step 1 – Raise Your Awareness

Step 2 – Align Your Consciousness

Step 3 – Activate Your Embodiment.

Forgive yourself for all the times you stepped over your inner knowing and being hard on yourself- it will open the door for your HEART TO SMILE again!

- Heather Passant

THIS AWESOME QUOTE FROM:

Heather Passant
Love, Courage and Relationship Coach
www.LifeHarmony.com.au

"

The Biggest Leap Of Faith Comes From Within – Leap As Often As You Can!

"

- Lynda Gale

THIS AWESOME QUOTE FROM:

Lynda Gale

www.3PConcepts.com.au

66

Sometimes the bravest thing you can do is allow yourself to love and be loved.

- Katrina Fox

99

THIS AWESOME QUOTE FROM:

Katrina Fox

www.KatrinaFox.com

> *Reveal YOUR awesomeness by unlocking the love and strength of YOUR soul so that YOUR mind, heart and spirit can soar in the Space of Total Possibilities.*
>
> - Lorraine Enright

THIS AWESOME QUOTE FROM:

Lorraine Enright

www.CertitudeLifeCoaching.com.au

> 66
>
> *The Universe only "knows" you as ENERGY. That ENERGY you feel in every cell for someone very special (or even your pet)... That's who you really are in your heart... pure LOVE. Be that energy - Be Love - you ARE awesome!*
>
> 99
>
> - Lyn Bowker

THIS AWESOME QUOTE FROM:

Lyn Bowker

www.AuthenticBusinessBuildingAcademy.com

"

Love deeply and believe completely, live boldly and forgive wholly, give unconditionally and receive gratefully, think freely and dream sweetly. Pray faithfully and act courageously, speak truthfully and listen openly, work joyfully.

"

- Anna Taylor

THIS AWESOME QUOTE FROM:

Joy T. Barican

www.facebook.com/JoyTBaricanEmceeServices

> *In life, you have the choice about how you create your business or work. So choose a business or work that supports your overall goals for life.*
>
> *Most won't but you're different!*

- William Siebler

THIS AWESOME QUOTE FROM:

William Siebler

www.SeoMelbourne1.com

> *Be the best you can be.*
> *Strive daily to develop your*
> *potential toward your*
> *higher being and in the*
> *process, lead the way for*
> *others to follow.*
>
> - Gaye O'Brien

THIS AWESOME QUOTE FROM:

Gaye O'Brien

www.GayeOBrien.com

66

When I feel down or unmotivated, when I feel like quitting or giving up, there are two persons that I always remember. They give me hope, they give me purpose, and they give me a reason to push on. These two persons are my Family and God.

99

- Kemar Harris

THIS AWESOME QUOTE FROM:

Kemar Harris

www.KemarHarris.com

> **"**
>
> *Freedom comes from living courageously with a kind and open heart and being UNRECOGNIZABLE to yourself each and every day!*
>
> **"**
>
> - Heather Passant

THIS AWESOME QUOTE FROM:

Heather Passant
Love, Courage and Relationship Coach
www.LifeHarmony.com.au

The world is full of nice people. If you can't find one…be one.

- Unknown

THIS AWESOME QUOTE FROM:

Liz Sayers

www.Lizz.JeunesseGlobal.com

"

I cannot give you the formula for success, but I can give you the formula for failure, which is: Try to please everybody.

"

- Herbert Swope

THIS AWESOME QUOTE FROM:

Herbert Swope

www.en.wikipedia.org/wiki/Herbert_Bayard_Swope

Download the

"Your Awesome Life!"

Mobile App

For 'on the go'
inspiration as well as:

Meditations to
'Activate Your Awesomeness' whenever
needed.

Available now at
iTunes, Google Play and Amazon app
stores

CHAPTER 5

Awesome EXPRESSION

DEFINITION:

EXPRESSION is your voice, your message, your sound and your words.

These quotes will give you an awareness and consciousness about the importance of communicating your truth and listening deeply to enjoy a more empowered, awesome way of expressing yourself.

THE
'YOUR AWESOME LIFE™'
ACTIVATION SYSTEM

Refer to the Introduction for full details.

Step 1 – Raise Your Awareness

Step 2 – Align Your Consciousness

Step 3 – Activate Your Embodiment.

> *When you're working with others – Just be YOU!*
>
> *Aiming for perfection – creates less connection!!*
>
> - Ramona Lever

THIS AWESOME QUOTE FROM:

Ramona Lever

www.RamonaLever.com

> **"**
>
> *Successful people are always looking for opportunities to help others. Unsuccessful people are always asking, 'What's in it for me?'*
>
> **"**
>
> - Brian Tracy

THIS AWESOME QUOTE FROM:

Brian Tracy

www.BrianTracy.com

> "
>
> *The Eight Wonders of the World*
> **To See*
> **To Hear*
> **To Touch*
> **To Taste*
> **To Feel*
> **To Laugh*
> **To Love*
> **& To Be Grateful.*
>
> "
>
> - Nikkiblu

THIS AWESOME QUOTE FROM:

Nikki Galagher

www.NikkiBluLifeLessons.com

> **"**
>
> *When we share our stories, the process not only transforms others, but ourselves.*
>
> **"**
>
> - Katrina Fox

THIS AWESOME QUOTE FROM:

Katrina Fox

www.KatrinaFox.com

" "

Without customers, you don't have a business. You have a hobby.

"

- Don Peppers & Martha Rogers

THIS AWESOME QUOTE FROM:

Don Peppers and Martha Rogers

www.PeppersAndRogersGroup.com

66

Never be afraid to speak in your own voice.

The people who listen have been searching just for you.

99

- Anne Maybus

THIS AWESOME QUOTE FROM:

Anne Maybus

www.CleverStreak.com

> **"**
>
> *With one voice we may whisper but with many we will roar.*
>
> **"**
>
> - Jackie Barreau

THIS AWESOME QUOTE FROM:

Jackie Barreau

www.JackieBarreau.com

> "
>
> *Write your own story.*
>
> *Don't let someone write it for you.*
>
> *Embrace it, live it and enjoy it!*
>
> "
>
> - Diahann C Ogunde

THIS AWESOME QUOTE FROM:

Diahann C Ogunde

www.fiverr.com/EditorWizard

"

Expect the best. Prepare for the worst. Capitalize on what comes.

"

- Zig Ziglar

THIS AWESOME QUOTE FROM:

Zig Ziglar

www.Ziglar.com

> *Expressing your truth is the gift that the world is waiting for from you.*
>
> *Your voice and words are important. Communicate them with conviction, compassion and love.*

- Trish Rock

THIS AWESOME QUOTE FROM:

Trish Rock

www.AwesomePublications.com

"

I was born of the Hebrew persuasion, but since joining the world of internet marketers, I've recently converted to … narcissism.

"

- Captain Lou Edwards

THIS AWESOME QUOTE FROM:

Captain Lou Edwards

www.ILoveJVs.com

"

I'm not a perfect friend. I am not a perfect mum. I am not a perfect wife. I am not a perfect person. I'm yet to find anyone that is. Until then, I will be me and do my best. I may get it wrong from time to time, but there's always room for improvement in everyone.

"

- Heather James

THIS AWESOME QUOTE FROM:

Heather James, Inspiring Mums®
"Where Mums Smile & Shine®"
www.inspiringmums.com.au

66

A lot of people will
disappoint you in life.

Don't let any of them be
you.

99

- Ian Williams

THIS AWESOME QUOTE FROM:

Ian Williams

www.facebook.com/IanWilliamsRealEstate

CHAPTER 6

Awesome VISION

DEFINITION:

VISION is connection. A channel of thought to higher self and inner knowing that will intuitively give you direction and answers.

These quotes will give you an awareness and consciousness about the importance of tuning in to your bigger visions and creating a more awesome connection to abundance in life.

**THE
'YOUR AWESOME LIFE™'
ACTIVATION SYSTEM**

Refer to the Introduction for full details.

Step 1 – Raise Your Awareness

Step 2 – Align Your Consciousness

Step 3 – Activate Your Embodiment.

66

The law of attraction equation is simple - you attract what you think about - so get proactive on making those thoughts good ones!

99

- Kat Mikic

THIS AWESOME QUOTE FROM:

Kat Mikic

www.KatMikic.com

> " "
>
> *Awesome happens   just let it.*
>
> " "
>
> - Roula

THIS AWESOME QUOTE FROM:

Roula

www.PicsByRoula.com

> **66**
>
> *You will never find balance in your life if you deny any part of your life or yourself.*
>
> *You get to own it all and only then is it possible to balance it all out!*
>
> **99**
>
> - Jen Appreneur

THIS AWESOME QUOTE FROM:

Jen Appreneur
Godmother Of Awesomeness
www.AwesomePublications.com

> **"**
>
> *Limitations live only in our minds. But if we use our imaginations, our possibilities become limitless.*
>
> **"**
>
> - Jamie Paolinetti

THIS AWESOME QUOTE FROM:

Jamie Paolinetti

www.dailypeloton.com/paol.asp

> ❝
>
> *Dreams come a size too big so that we can grow into them.*
>
> ❞
>
> - Author Unknown

THIS AWESOME QUOTE FROM:

Lisa Bowen

www.ElisiTherapies.com.au

> 66
>
> *A leader is a person you will follow to a place you wouldn't go by yourself.*
>
> 99
>
> - Joel Barker

THIS AWESOME QUOTE FROM:

Joel Barker

www.JoelBarker.com

"

The most trusting voice you can ever listen to is that one you hear first.

"

- Trish Rock

THIS AWESOME QUOTE FROM:

Trish Rock

www.StrategicBusinessApps.com

> ❝
>
> *The minute you're satisfied with where you are, you aren't there anymore.*
>
> ❞
>
> - Tony Gwynn

THIS AWESOME QUOTE FROM:

Tony Gwynn

www.en.wikipedia.org/wiki/Tony_Gwynn

> 66
>
> *The person who abandons taking responsibility for determining the direction of their mind will fall off life's cliffs, but those who invest in their mind will climb every mountain.*
>
> 99
>
> - Tracie O'Keefe

THIS AWESOME QUOTE FROM:

Tracie O'Keefe

www.DoctorOK.com

> " Build your own dreams, or someone else will hire you to build theirs. "
>
> - Farrah Gray

THIS AWESOME QUOTE FROM:

Farrah Gray

www.FarrahGray.com

66

Motherhood is a lifetime commitment. With its many twists and turns, ups and downs, mothers have the inherent ability to ride the waves, brave the storms and dare to bounce back with a vengeance!

99

- Heather James

THIS AWESOME QUOTE FROM:

Heather James, Inspiring Mums®
"Where Mums Smile & Shine®"
www.InspiringMums.com.au

> **"**
>
> *Strive not to be a success,*
> *but rather to be of value.*
>
> **"**
>
> - Albert Einstein

THIS AWESOME QUOTE FROM:

Albert Einstein

www.Einstein.biz

"

If you can dream it, you can achieve it.

"

- Zig Ziglar

THIS AWESOME QUOTE FROM:

Zig Ziglar

www.Ziglar.com

CHAPTER 7

Awesome KNOWING

DEFINITION:

KNOWING is your energy/source connection to all things. Your gateway to enlightenment and the feeling of oneness in all life comes from this flow of energy.

These quotes will give you an awareness and consciousness about the importance of this connection for a more awesome universal perception.

THE
'YOUR AWESOME LIFE™'
ACTIVATION SYSTEM

Refer to the Introduction for full details.

Step 1 – Raise Your Awareness

Step 2 – Align Your Consciousness

Step 3 – Activate Your Embodiment.

> 66
>
> *DREAMS are not just the unconscious babblings of your mind as you sleep. When you connect to your internal, eternal power source, dreams are the reality YOU CREATE in each moment. MAGIC DOES HAPPEN when you try on your dream.*
>
> 99
>
> - Kirsty Greenshields

THIS AWESOME QUOTE FROM:

Kirsty Greenshields

www.WomenMoneyAndIntimacy.com

> *It's not the years in your life that count. It's the life in your years.*
>
> - Abraham Lincoln

THIS AWESOME QUOTE FROM:

Abraham Lincoln

www.AbrahamLincolnOnline.org

66

Only those who can see the invisible are able to do what seems to be impossible.

99

- Kemar Harris

THIS AWESOME QUOTE FROM:

Kemar Harris

www.KemarHarris.com

> "
>
> *My ego thinks it's me.*
>
> "
>
> - Frank Topper

THIS AWESOME QUOTE FROM:

Frank Topper

www.TopperFacilitation.com

66

My life journey is one of discovery, independence, fulfillment and completion.

I already possess access to all the answers I need simply by sitting quietly and listening, with trust, to the messages delivered within.

99

- Jen Appreneur

THIS AWESOME QUOTE FROM:

Jen Appreneur
Godmother Of Awesomeness
www.AwesomePublications.com

"

The common question that gets asked in business is 'why?'

That's a good question, but an equally valid one is 'why not?'

"

- Jeffrey Bezos

THIS AWESOME QUOTE FROM:

Jeffrey Bezos

http://en.wikipedia.org/wiki/Jeff_Bezos

66

Beyond is where Surprises lay, and Greatness is achieved.

99

- Batia Grinblat

THIS AWESOME QUOTE FROM:

Batia Grinblat

www.InnerEnlightenmentPtyLtd.com

We all have an inner knowing, a 'remembrance' of who we are and of the source energy that runs through us and through all life.

Trust it, know it, and allow the flow of light.

- Trish Rock

THIS AWESOME QUOTE FROM:

Trish Rock

www.AwesomePublications.com

"

Your belief is standing between you and your awesomeness.

Change your thought, change your life, live your dream!

"

- Anoushka Gungadin

THIS AWESOME QUOTE FROM:

Anoushka Gungadin

www.Leaderpreneur.com.au

"

Great ideas often receive violent opposition from mediocre minds.

"

- Albert Einstein

THIS AWESOME QUOTE FROM:

Albert Einstein

www.Einstein.biz

> ❝
>
> *Being truly awesome is everyone's gift to themselves and the world...*
>
> *Some people just take a lot longer to unwrap the present!*
>
> ❞
>
> - Andrea Dix

THIS AWESOME QUOTE FROM:

Andrea Dix

www.IronButterfly.com.au

> **"**
>
> *The promise of a flower lives within every seed and within each of us lies the ability to lead an extraordinary life.*
>
> **"**
>
> - Debbie Ford

THIS AWESOME QUOTE FROM:

Heather Passant
Love, Courage and Relationship Coach
www.LifeHarmony.com.au

Download the

"Your Awesome Life!"

Mobile App

For 'on the go'
inspiration as well as:

Meditations to
'Activate Your Awesomeness' whenever
needed.

Available now at
iTunes, Google Play and Amazon app
stores

BIBLIOGRAPHY

Name

APPRENEUR, Jen
www.AwesomePublications.com
www.QueendomOfWealth.com

ARISTOTLE
www.en.wikipedia.org/wiki/Aristotle

ASH, Arthur
www.en.wikipedia.org/wiki/Arthur_Ashe

BARREAU, Jackie
www.JackieBarreau.com

BARICAN, Joy T.
www.facebook.com/JoyTBaricanEmceeServices

BARKER, Joel
www.JoelBarker.com

BOWEN, Lisa
www.ElisiTherapies.com.au

BOWKER, Lyn
www.AuthenticBusinessBuildingAcademy.com

CAMDEN-BURCH, Claire
www.facebook.com/AlignmentAffirmations

CHANSAMOOTH, Anfernee
www.Confidentpreneur.com

CONNOLLY, Allan
www.BigAlConnolly.info

COPPENS, An
www.GamificationNation.com

CROSBIE, Maree
www.MareeCrosbie.com

DANGERFIELD, Phoebe
www.MindBizNiz.com.au

DIX, Andrea
www.IronButterfly.com,au

EDWARDS, John
www.ParentConsciously.com

EDWARDS, Lou
www.ILoveJVs.com

EINSTEIN, Albert
www.en.wikipedia.org/wiki/Albert_einstein

ENRIGHT, Lorraine
www.CertitudeLifeCoaching.com.au

FOX, Katrina
www.KatrinaFox.com

GALAGHER, Nikki
www.NikkiBluLifeLessons.com

GALE, Lynda
www.3pconcepts.com.au

GEORGOPOULOS, Chris
www.DiscoveringYourInnerGem.com

GIBBONS, Melissa
www.AngelicEarth.com.au

GRAY, Farrah
www.FarrahGray.com

GREENSHIELDS, Kirsty
www.WomenMoneyAndIntimacy.com

GRINBLAT, Batia
www.InnerEnlightenmentPtyLtd.com

GUNGADIN, Anoushka
www.Leaderpreneur.com.au

GWYNN, Tony
www.en.wikipedia.org/wiki/Tony_gwynn

HALL, Ana
www.AnaHall.wordpress.com

HAMEL, Gary
www.GaryHamel.com

HARRIS, Kemar
www.KemarHarris.com

HELLIWELL, Georgina
www.facebook.com/AnimalAlchemy

HOLMES, Kathie
www.CreativeAbilityNetwork.com

JAMES, Heather
www.InspiringMums.com.au

KLIPSCH, Jutta
juttaklipsch@gmail.com

LEVER, Ramona
www.RamonaLever.com

LINCOLN, Abraham
www.en.wikipedia.org/wiki/Abraham_lincoln

MAHONY, Donna
www.Innatepd.com

MAYBUS, Anne
www.CleverStreak.com

McSHANE, Tryphena
www.IntimacyOfDeathAndDying.com

MIKIC, Kat
www.KatMikic.com

O'BRIEN, Gaye
www.GayeOBrien.com

OGUNDE, Diahann C
www.fiverr.com/EditorWizard

O'KEEFE, Tracie
www.DoctorOK.com

PAOLINETTI, Jamie
www.dailypeloton.com/paol.asp

PASSANT, Heather
www.LifeHarmony.com.au

PEPPERS, Don
www.PeppersAndRogersGroup.com

PERROW, Emma
www.SimpleFitness.com.au

POLLOCK, Cheryl
www.LiveLaughLoveCoaching.com.au

ROBBINS, Tony
www.TonyRobbins.com

ROBSON, Melissa
www.DivineCreative.com.au

ROCK, Trish
www.AwesomePublications.com
www.StrategicBusinessApps.com

ROGERS, Martha
www.PeppersAndRogersGroup.com

ROULA, Roula
www.PicsByRoula.com

SAYERS, Liz
www.Lizz.JeunesseGlobal.com

SIEBLER, William
www.SEOMelbourne1.com

SMITH, Leisa Hunter
www.LeisaSmith.com

STONE, W. Clement
www.en.wikipedia.org/wiki/W._Clement_Stone

SWOPE, Herbert
www.en.wikipedia.org/wiki/Herbert_Swope

TOPPER, Frank
www.TopperFacilitation.com

TORRENS, Nicole
www.NicoleTorrens.com

TRACY, Brian
www.BrianTracy.com

USHER, Sam
www.AdventurePhilosopher.com

WILLIAMS, Ian
www.facebook.com/IanWilliamsRealEstate

ZIGLER, Zig
www.Ziglar.com

OTHER RESOURCES

- **Join our "Awesome Source" Mail list (90 Days <u>FREE</u> Membership)**

Go to www.AwesomeSourceNews.com to join now!

- **Download the "Awesome Life" App**

Search "Awesome Life" or "Your Awesome Life" in iTunes, Google Play and Amazon app stores.

- **Download the "Awesome Life Activation Meditations"**

Details on how to do that are included in the app.

- **Join the "Year of Living Awesomely" Facebook Community**

Go to www.facebook.com/groups/awesomelife.

- **Join our Facebook Page**

Connect with us at www.facebook.com/AwesomeLife.

- **Become An Author/Contributor**

Visit us at www.AwesomePublications.com.

- **Advertise In the App**

Send an email via info@awesomepublications.com.

- **Media inquiries**

Send an email via info@awesomepublications.com.

www.ingramcontent.com/pod-product-compliance
Lightning Source LLC
Chambersburg PA
CBHW061739020426
42331CB00006B/1290